W9-DDE-787

Planets and Moons

Giles Sparrow

WORLD ALMANAC® LIBRARY

Please visit our Web site at: www.garethstevens.com
For a free color catalog describing World Almanac® Library's list of high-quality books
and multimedia programs, call 1-800-848-2928 (USA) or 1-800-387-3178 (Canada).
World Almanac® Library's fax: (414) 332-3567.

Library of Congress Cataloging-in-Publication Data

Sparrow, Giles.
     Planets and moons / by Giles Sparrow.
        p. cm. — (Secrets of the universe)
     Includes bibliographical references and index.
     ISBN-10: 0-8368-7278-9 — ISBN-13: 978-0-8368-7278-1 (lib. bdg.)
     ISBN-10: 0-8368-7285-1 — ISBN-13: 978-0-8368-7285-9 (softcover)
   1. Planets—Juvenile literature. 2. Satellites—Juvenile literature. I. Title.
II. Series: Sparrow, Giles. Secrets of the universe. III. Series.
   QB602.S68   2007
   523.4—dc22   2006009959

This North American edition first published in 2007 by
World Almanac® Library
A Member of the WRC Media Family of Companies
330 West Olive Street, Suite 100
Milwaukee, WI 53212 USA

This U.S. edition copyright © 2007 by World Almanac® Library. Original edition copyright
© 2006 by IMP. FProduced by Amber Books Ltd., Bradley's Close, 74–77 White Lion Street,
London N1 9PF, U.K.

Amber Books project editor: James Bennett
Amber Books design: Richard Mason
Amber Books picture research: Terry Forshaw

World Almanac® Library editor: Carol Ryback
World Almanac® Library designer: Scott M. Krall
World Almanac® Library art direction: Tammy West
World Almanac® Library production: Jessica Morris and Robert Kraus

Picture acknowledgments: All photographs courtesy of NASA except for the following:
Getty Images: 15 (Johner Images); 37 (Stock Montage). Topfoto: 9.
All artworks courtesy of International Masters Publishers Ltd.

Printed in the United States of America

1 2 3 4 5 6 7 8 9 10 09 08 07 06

CONTENTS

PLANETS AND MOONS   4

THE EARTH AND ITS MOON   12

EXTREME ENVIRONMENTS   22

AMONG THE GIANTS   30

MINOR WORLDS   38

GLOSSARY   46

FURTHER INFORMATION   47

INDEX   48

Cover and title page: Dione, one of Saturn's eighteen moons, not only is littered with impact craters, but also shares its orbital path with another, smaller moon. The appearance of Saturn's rings from Earth changes gradually over roughly fifteen years as the gas giant rotates on its axis.

CHAPTER 1

PLANETS AND MOONS

What is a planet? At one time, this question had a simple answer—the planets were five wandering objects in the sky that moved against the background stars. Named after Roman gods and goddesses, the five planets of the ancients were Mercury, Venus, Mars, Jupiter, and Saturn. Most early astronomers recognized that these planets, along with the Moon and Sun, were much closer than the "fixed" stars. Until the sixteenth century, however, the most popular theory to explain them was that they were objects attached to a series of transparent spheres centered around Earth. In the early 1600s, a revolution in open-minded thinking occurred, and—along with the development of scientific instruments—the truth became apparent: Earth and all the other planets orbited the Sun on elliptical paths.

With the birth of the telescope, astronomers saw the disks and surface features of the planets for the first time. Jupiter, Saturn, and eventually, Mars, turned out to have smaller worlds, classed as satellites, or moons, orbiting them. Then in 1781, William Herschel discovered Uranus, the first new planet, and the size of the solar system doubled in an instant. Early observers became confused in the early 1800s, when they started finding small objects orbiting between Mars and Jupiter. At first these were classed as planets, but when it became obvious that there were thousands of them, and that most were very small, a new term—asteroids—was coined.

Discovered in 1846, Neptune was clearly a planet on the same scale as Uranus. But disturbances in its orbit led astronomers to believe there must be another world beyond it, and so the search began. Pluto, discovered in 1930, has been the most troublesome "planet" of all. As the smallest known planet, it seemed out of place at the

In an image captured by *Voyager 2* in 1979, the moon Io passes above Jupiter's stormy southern hemisphere.

edge of the solar system until, in the 1990s, astronomers began discovering other worlds in similar orbits circulating in the far-out "Kuiper Belt" region. Then, in 2003, they found an object larger than Pluto. Are all of these objects planets—or is Pluto not a planet?

It is very difficult to use one definition to describe all the planets. Whatever we decide is correct, the definition will always leave out one of the traditional "nine" planets or include other objects that we don't want. Nevertheless, the subjects of this book include the planets, their moons, and all the other objects that form the solar system—the countless worlds, large and small, orbiting the star we call the Sun.

Orbits of the planets

The area of space dominated by our Sun's gravity is called the solar system. Its outer limits are estimated to lie more than 1 light-year (roughly 6 trillion miles or 10 trillion kilometers) from the Sun. Most of this is empty space, and the region occupied by the planets is tiny in comparison. For example, the outer edge of Pluto's orbit takes it 4.6 billion miles (7.4 billion km) from the Sun. All of the outer planets lie much closer to the Sun.

Mercury, smaller than any planet except for Pluto, is the closest to the Sun. It has an 88-day orbit that resembles a circle that has been stretched slightly (known as an elliptical orbit). Its average distance from the Sun is 36 million miles (58 million km). Mercury's orbit is also tilted at seven degrees from the general plane (or "ecliptic") of the solar system.

Venus, the second planet, is almost the same size as Earth. It has a more circular orbit than Mercury, with an average distance of 67 million miles (108 million km) from the Sun. Venus orbits the Sun once every 225 Earth days.

Because they lie closer to the Sun than Earth, Mercury and Venus are known as "inferior" planets. Their orbits can only take them a certain distance from the Sun in the sky, and they are generally seen east of the Sun after sunset, or

Sun

Jupiter

Earth

Venus

Mars

Mercury

Pluto

Neptune

Uranus

Saturn

While the size-scale of the major objects in the solar system appear fairly accurate here, the scale of orbits is not. Our star dwarfs all the planets, yet Jupiter itself could swallow up every other planet in the solar system with ease.

THE ELECTROMAGNETIC SPECTRUM

Light that we see is only a small part of the electromagnetic (EM) spectrum—the mostly invisible radiation, or energy, given off by stars. Electromagnetic radiation takes the form of different wavelengths of energy as it travels across the universe. All wavelengths of the EM spectrum move at the same speed: the speed of light—186,000 miles (300,000 km) per second.

The visible part of the EM spectrum, in the middle, ranges from red light—with longer wavelengths—to violet light—with shorter wavelengths. Beyond the visible violet light, the wavelengths become increasingly short, high-energy wavelengths that give off dangerous ionizing, or "hot," radiation such as ultraviolet rays, X-rays, and gamma rays. Likewise, the wavelengths beyond red light become increasingly long, with lower energy levels, such as infrared (heat) waves, microwaves, radar waves, and radio waves.

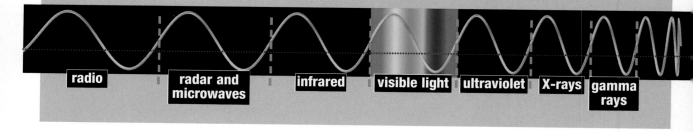

radio | radar and microwaves | infrared | visible light | ultraviolet | X-rays | gamma rays

west of the Sun before sunrise. We see different amounts of their sunlit surfaces at different points in their orbits. When studied with a telescope, these planets show phases similar to the phases of the Moon.

Earth itself is the solar system's third planet. It orbits at an average distance of 93 million miles (150 million km) from the Sun, rotates once every 23 hours 56 minutes, and takes 365.25 days to complete one orbit (*see page 14*). We are accompanied on our journey through space by a comparatively huge natural satellite, the Moon. Almost the size of Mercury, the Moon has had a great effect on our planet's development.

Mars is considerably smaller than Earth, and is the last of four rocky, or "terrestrial," planets. Its elliptical orbit takes it from perihelion—its closest approach to the Sun (128 million miles/205 million km), to aphelion—its greatest distance from the Sun (155 million miles/250 million km). It also has two tiny moons, Phobos and Deimos (their names come from the Greek for "fear" and

Mars has striking similarities to Earth—its tilted axis and rotation period are almost the same, and it even has striking white ice caps at its poles. The northern ice cap is clearly visible in this image.

"dread," respectively). These are probably asteroids that were caught by the gravitational pull of Mars and now orbit around it.

The outer planets

Beyond the asteroid belt that circles Mars's orbit, lie the gas giant planets: Jupiter, Saturn, Uranus, and Neptune—all far larger than any of the terrestrial worlds. Jupiter, with an atmosphere wracked by violent storms, is the largest of these. It has a system of several dozen moons, dominated by four "Galilean" satellites, each very different from the other, and all about the size of Mercury. Jupiter orbits at an average distance of 484 million miles (778 million km) from the Sun, and its orbit takes roughly twelve years.

Saturn is a smaller, paler version of Jupiter, orbiting at 840 million miles (1.4 billion km) from the Sun, once every twenty-nine years. Its famous and spectacular ring system consists of tiny ice and rock particles in separate orbits around the planet itself. All the other giant planets have rings, but none come close to the beauty of Saturn's. The sixth planet also has a huge family of moons, including Titan—a world thought to resemble Earth in its early history.

Uranus and Neptune are nearly twins. Both are blue-green "ice giants" with about four times the diameter of Earth and large families of moons. Uranus rotates "on its side" when compared to the other planets and at an average distance of 1.8 billion miles (2.9 billion km) over 84 Earth years. Neptune orbits at 2.8 billion miles (4.5 billion km) over 165 Earth years.

Pluto, the last widely recognized planet, is the tiniest of all. Astronomers now believe that Pluto is actually the most prominent member of the Kuiper Belt of small, icy worlds. Its 249-year orbit is wildly eccentric, moving from 2.8 billion miles (4.5 billion km) at perihelion to 4.6 billion miles (7.4 billion km) at aphelion. At times, Pluto moves in closer to the Sun than Neptune. Pluto's orbit is also tilted at an angle of 17 degrees to the plane of the solar system.

JOHANNES KEPLER

German astronomer Johannes Kepler (1571–1630) finally solved the mystery of planetary orbits in 1609. Until 1543, when Nicolaus Copernicus (1743–1543) put forth his idea that the Sun was the center of the solar system, most astronomers considered Earth the center of the solar system, with the Sun, Moon, and planets moving around it. But even Copernicus believed

that the planets moved along perfectly circular paths. Kepler used highly precise measurements of the planets made by Danish astronomer Tycho Brahe (1546–1601) to determine how the planets moved. He realized for the first time that the orbits were stretched ellipses rather than circles, and that the speed of a planet along its orbit increased when it was closer to the Sun.

Johannes Kepler was not only a pioneering astronomer, but also a mystic and astrologer at a time when science was not so clearly defined.

Countless smaller worlds are moving in orbit between and beyond the planets. In this region, we find rocky asteroids close to the Sun and icy comets that spend most of their time in the outer solar system. Beyond even the Kuiper Belt, at the limits of where the Sun's gravity reaches, lies the Oort Cloud, a great reservoir of a trillion or more comets.

Formation of the Solar System

The solar system was formed from material left over when the Sun was born. Bearing this fact in mind, astronomers have been able to relate different zones of the solar system and the different types of objects in it to the "solar nebula" from which everything was created.

The Sun was born when a large cloud of gas and dust began collapsing about five billion years ago. As the center of the cloud got heavier, its gravity pulled in more nearby material. As the core of the cloud grew denser, it heated up. Conditions in the heart of this collapsing cloud eventually became so hot and dense that nuclear fusion could occur, and the Sun began to shine.

Meanwhile, material in the solar nebula around the Sun continued to collapse, forming a flattened disk rotating around the Sun. This material was a mixture of gas, dust, and chemical "ices"—materials that would melt and turn into gas at relatively low temperatures. The fierce radiation from the young Sun was enough to evaporate many of these ices and blow away most of the gas in the inner region, leaving mostly dust particles behind. As these began to collide and stick together (or "accrete"), the larger ones formed into the beginnings of planets with enough gravity to pull in more material from around them. Within a few million years, there were several dozen of these so-called "protoplanets," which then collided and merged together to form the planets we know today.

Farther out in the cloud, away from the fierce heat, gas and ice survived alongside the dust. It seems that instabilities in the nebula created four separate, slowly collapsing clouds that formed the giant planets. Ice and dust not absorbed by the planets themselves formed miniature accretion disks around them,

OBSERVING ACROSS THE SPECTRUM

Only a small fraction of electromagnetic (EM) radiation from space reaches the surface of Earth. Although our planet's atmosphere absorbs most of the ultraviolet (UV) and some of the infrared (IR) and radio wavelengths, the visible portion of the EM spectrum makes it to the ground intact. We feel the IR radiation that penetrates the atmosphere as the Sun's heat on our bodies and other objects, while the UV rays that get through often produce skin damage, including tanning or sunburn. Still, the atmosphere also protects us from the more dangerous and damaging EM wavelengths, including X-rays and gamma rays.

We use the different wavelengths of the EM spectrum to explore space. Most ground-based telescopes scan the universe using visible light. For the clearest views, they are often located on mountaintops, where Earth's atmosphere is thinnest. On these mountain peaks, special IR telescopes also detect some of the IR radiation before the denser parts of our atmosphere block it. The best IR observing occurs from space-based telescopes, not only because of the lack of atmospheric blocking, but also because of the lack of ambient heat generated by Earth and by the IR telescope itself—which can distort images. The cold temperatures of space also require less refrigerant for cooling an orbiting IR telescope.

Earth-based radio telescopes, like the famous one in Arecibo, Puerto Rico, consist of huge metal dishes that collect long-wavelength radio

A protoplanet plows through the solar nebula and sweeps up surrounding material during the early days of the solar system.

collapsing to form moons that are a mixture of ice and dust.

Toward the outer edge of the solar system, the nebula grew sparse. Here, dust and ice accreted to form ice dwarf worlds, such as Pluto. Collisions between these objects rarely occurred. Some evidence indicates that the gas giants actually formed farther out from the Sun in the same region as comets and ice dwarfs. Encounters between the gas giants and the smaller worlds flung many of the latter out to the edge of the solar system to form the Oort Cloud as the gas giants slowly spiraled inward to their present positions.

waves from space. Smaller versions of radio telescopes, often built in movable groups called arrays, allow astronomers to combine many separate radio images into one larger image. Additionally, space-based radio telescopes collect and beam such data to Earth.

Space-based telescopes capable of studying the universe in different wavelengths became a reality in the decades after the launch of *Sputnik,* the world's first artificial satellite. While the famous *Hubble Space Telescope (HST)* collects images in visible light, it also carries equipment that scans the universe in IR—as does the *Spitzer Space Telescope (Spitzer).* Space-based UV instruments include the *Hopkins Ultraviolet Telescope,* used by space shuttle astronauts, the *Cosmic Hot Interstellar Plasma Spectrometer (CHIPS),* and the *Far Ultraviolet Spectroscopic Explorer (FUSE)* Mission. The *Wilkinson Microwave Anisotropy Probe (WMAP)* studies and maps the background microwave radiation of the universe. Space-based X-ray detectors include the *Rossi X-ray Timing Explorer* Mission, and the *XMM-Newton* and *Chandra* X-ray observatories, while the *High Energy Transient Explorer-2 (HETE-2)* Mission and *International Gamma-Ray Astrophysics Laboratory (INTEGRAL)* detect gamma-ray wavelengths. Telescopes dedicated to short-wavelength EM radiation are built to prevent these high-energy rays from simply passing right through them.

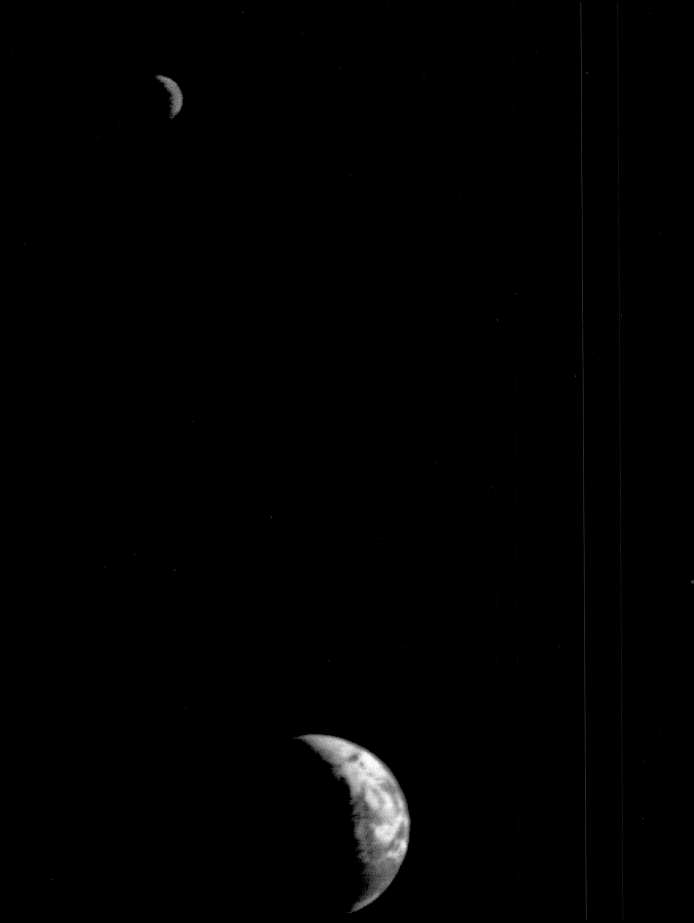

CHAPTER 2

THE EARTH AND ITS MOON

The Earth is unique in the solar system as the only planet able to support abundant life. Its size and position in the solar system combine to make it particularly hospitable. It is also a very active world, with slowly drifting continental plates, volcanic activity, and liquid oceans. Earth's "water cycle" constantly reshapes land surfaces through erosion. Earth's Moon is a giant compared with its parent planet (only Pluto's satellite Charon is larger in comparison), and the Earth and Moon have influenced each other throughout their histories.

Planet Earth

With a diameter of 7,926 miles (12,756 km), Earth is slightly larger than its next-door neighbor Venus, and orbits slightly farther from the Sun. The crucial factor that makes our planet so unique is the ability for water to exist in three different states on its surface—as liquid, solid (ice), and gas (water vapor). This is partly because Earth's gravity is strong enough to hold onto a substantial atmosphere which protects it from violent changes in temperature, but mostly because Earth happens to lie in the middle of the solar system's "Goldilocks" or "habitable zone," where conditions are neither too hot nor too cold for life as we know it.

Water is constantly melting from the poles, evaporating from the oceans, and falling from the sky as precipitation (either snow or rain). This constant circulation of liquid through the environment not only shapes and erodes the landscape but also changes the very nature of the rocks themselves.

Earth's size also means that it is large enough to retain a molten interior—the other main force behind Earth's changing surface. Although only the core (occupying roughly one-quarter of Earth's diameter) is

The first-ever picture of Earth and its Moon in a single frame. The *Voyager 1* spacecraft captured this image on September 18, 1977, when it was 7 million miles (12 million km) from Earth.

molten, the mantle that surrounds it is made of semimolten rocks that push past each other and carry heat slowly from the core to the surface. Earth's solid crust is a thin layer, ranging between 4 miles (7 km) thick on the ocean floors to 45 miles (70 km) beneath the continents. Movement of the underlying mantle has caused the crust to split into a number of large and small "tectonic plates," which float around on top of the mantle, moving at speeds of 1 inch (2.5 centimeters) or so each year. Although the plates are slow, they are almost unstoppable: Where they collide with each other, mountain ranges form; where one is forced beneath another, chains of volcanoes form; and where they are pulled apart (mostly beneath Earth's oceans), volcanic rift valleys create new rock to fill the gaps.

Earth's seasons

Like many of the other planets, Earth experiences seasons. These result from changes in the amount of sunlight and heat reaching different parts of the planet's surface, caused by the tilt of the planet's axis of rotation. Earth's axis is tilted at 23.5 degrees from "straight up." For one half of the year, the Northern Hemisphere is more exposed to the Sun than the Southern Hemisphere; for the other half, the situation is reversed. On about June 21st, when the North Pole is pointing toward the Sun, the northern days are longest and it is northern midsummer (even though Earth is actually at its greatest distance from the Sun at this point in its orbit). On about December 21st, the Southern Hemisphere gets maximum sunlight, and the Northern Hemisphere gets the least. The changes in the length of day and their effects on the climate become more extreme toward the poles. The equator gets roughly the same amount of sunlight throughout the entire year.

Giant satellite

Earth's Moon is huge—at some 2,159 miles (3,475 km) in diameter, it is only slightly smaller than the planet Mercury. It orbits Earth at an

THE SPEED OF LIGHT

All electromagnetic (EM) radiation travels through the vacuum of space at exactly the same speed—186,000 miles (300,000 km) per second. Most often, we call this the speed of light. (What we call "light" is the visible portion of the radiation of different wavelengths that makeup the EM spectrum.)

In his 1905 Special Theory of Relativity, Einstein's famous equation mathematically proved that nothing could travel faster than the speed of light. For this reason, we use the speed of light as a "constant"—a unit that never changes. One light-year is the distance light travels in one Earth year, which is roughly 6 trillion miles (10 trillion km). It is a convenient way of measuring the huge distances in space. In other words, a light-year measures distances, not time.

TIME AND THE CALENDAR

Our calendar and time systems compensate for various oddities about Earth's orbit and rotation periods. The Earth takes roughly 365.25 days to complete one orbit around the Sun, which we simplify to 365 days in most years. We make up for the extra one-quarter day every four years by adding an extra day, February 29, which make that year 366 days long. A 366-day year is known as a leap year.

Every fourth year is a leap year. Most centennial years—unless divisible by four—are not. The year 2000 was indeed a leap year.

average distance of 238,800 miles (384,400 km), and appears roughly the same size as the Sun in our sky. The Moon's mass is just one percent of Earth's, and its gravity is one-sixth that of Earth's. As a result, the Moon has not been able to hold onto an atmosphere. Without this protection, temperatures on the lunar surface vary from about 230 °Fahrenheit (110 °Celsius) during the lunar day to −275 °F (−170 °C) during the lunar night. The lack of an atmosphere also means that erosion on the Moon's surface is caused by the impact of meteorites. As a result, the lunar surface is a time capsule that reveals the Moon's entire history.

The Earth and Moon exert tidal forces on each other, and these have long ago slowed the Moon's rotation so that it spins on its axis in exactly the same time it takes to orbit the Earth. As a result, the Moon keeps one face permanently toward Earth (the near side), and another permanently hidden (the far side). The amount of the Earth-facing side we can see at any time depends on the angle between the

The Moon sometimes appears huge when low on the horizon. It's an optical illusion caused by atmospheric refraction.

Moon and Sun in Earth's skies. As a result, the Moon goes through a series of phases, from new Moon (when the sunlit side is entirely hidden from Earth), through crescent, first quarter (when half the sunlit side is visible), and gibbous, to full Moon (when the near side is in full sunlight), and back to new. This "lunar month" takes 29.5 days to complete. The Moon also receives some sunlight reflected off Earth. As a result, the entire disk of the Moon can often be seen glowing dimly with "Earthshine" around the time of the new Moon.

Because the Moon and Sun appear to be the same size in Earth's skies, they can create spectacular eclipses. Solar eclipses happen at new Moon, when the Moon happens to pass directly

ORIGINS OF THE MOON

For years, astronomers argued about the origin of the Moon. One theory held that the young Earth spun so quickly that a huge chunk of material flew off from the equator to form our satellite. Another stated that the Moon formed as a separate, small body resembling a planet, and was captured by Earth's gravity. Both theories had good and bad points. Rock samples brought back to Earth by the Apollo missions confused things even more. The lunar rocks display startling similarities to rocks on Earth—as well as important differences.

Today, the origin of the Moon remains a mystery, although most astronomers agree with a hypothesis called the giant impact theory, or "Big Splash." According to this, early in Earth's history, a huge protoplanet the size of Mars collided with Earth. The incoming planet was vaporized, along with a substantial amount of Earth's crust and mantle. While Earth stabilized and reformed itself, material flung out by the force of the collision formed a ring around the planet, which soon fused to form a new world—the Moon.

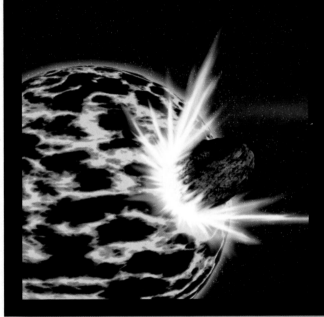

An artist's impression of the "Big Splash," which probably happened while Earth's surface was still semi-molten. Astronomers named the colliding protoplanet "Theia" after the mother of the Greek moon goddess, Selene.

in front of the Sun. The brilliant disk of the Sun is briefly blocked off, and the corona (the thin outer atmosphere of the Sun) becomes visible. Because the Moon blocks such a small portion of the sun's light, a total solar eclipse is only visible from a small region of Earth—the surrounding areas see only a partial eclipse. Lunar eclipses occur at full Moon, when the system is reversed, and Earth's shadow falls on the Moon. Lunar eclipses are more common. They often make the Moon appear blood red, because Earth's atmosphere acts like a giant lens, bending red light from the Sun onto the Moon's surface.

Surface of the Moon

Even with the naked eye, it's easy to tell that the Moon's surface has two distinct types of terrain—a brighter background and scattered darker patches. Looking through binoculars or a small telescope reveals even more detail. For

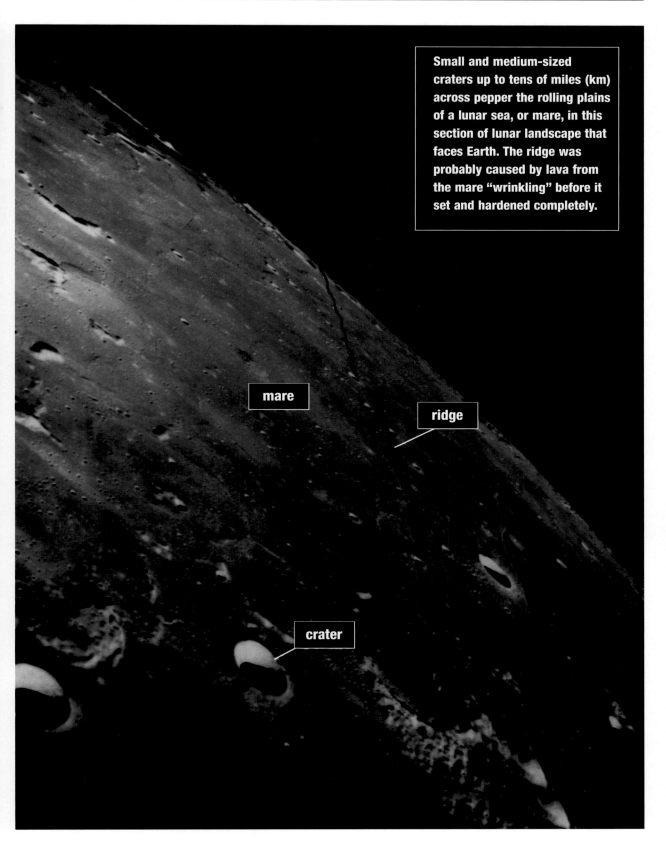

Small and medium-sized craters up to tens of miles (km) across pepper the rolling plains of a lunar sea, or mare, in this section of lunar landscape that faces Earth. The ridge was probably caused by lava from the mare "wrinkling" before it set and hardened completely.

mare

ridge

crater

example, the bright areas are covered in circular craters, while the darker areas tend to have far fewer craters. Early astronomers named the dark areas maria (from the Latin for seas—singular mare). They called the bright areas highlands. As the angle of sunlight hitting the Moon changes throughout the month, more features, such as mountains chains around the edge of the maria and ripples across their dark surfaces, appear. From Earth, the best lunar detail is visible during the crescent Moon stage.

Astronomers argued for centuries about the origins of the lunar craters. At one time, the idea of impacts from space was unheard of, so most people thought the craters must be volcanic in origin. The dispute was finally settled when the first lunar space probes revealed that the surface is covered with craters down to the tiniest size. It seems that the Moon, with has no atmosphere to protect it, has been a cosmic target throughout its history. It has retained a perfect record of every impact because there is no water or tectonic plates to reshape its surface.

But what about the maria, the lunar seas? Astronomers can tell that they are younger than the highlands because they have far fewer craters—clearly some event must have wiped them clean in the distant past. Clues to the nature of this event include the fact that the seas are positioned in low-lying regions of the surface, have wrinkled ridges, and volcanic "basalt" rocks dominate their surfaces. In fact, the lunar seas were once liquid, in the form of huge lakes of molten lava that erupted from inside the Moon and flooded its low-lying areas.

Rock samples brought back by astronauts helped reveal when and how this happened. An event 3.9 billion years ago called the "late heavy bombardment" soaked up most of the remaining debris floating around the inner solar system. Many of the lunar craters date to this time, including the huge "impact basins" where most of the maria lie. It seems that shortly after these giant craters formed (or perhaps as a result of them), lava erupted through huge cracks in the

lunar surface, flooding out across the lower-lying regions, and eventually cooling and solidifying into a new surface.

Curiously, the two halves of the Moon have very different surfaces. While the near side is split roughly evenly between seas and highlands, the far side is dominated by cratered highlands, with only a handful of small seas. As we shall see,

MAPPING THE MOON

Italian astronomer Galileo Galilei (1564–1642) and others drew the first maps of the Moon shortly after the invention of the telescope in about 1608. Galileo also named the system of "seas" and other features that dominate the lunar near side. Since the Moon rocks slightly from side to side as it tilts on its axis during orbit, we can map nearly 58 percent of the lunar surface from Earth.

In 1959, we got our first view of the Moon's far side thanks to the Soviet *Lunik 3* space probe, so many features on the far side have Russian names. A fleet of lunar orbiter spacecraft surveyed the Moon in preparation for the Apollo missions of the late 1960s. Among other achievements, they confirmed the existence of the "South Pole-Aitken Basin"—the largest known crater in the solar system—near the lunar south pole. More recently, space probes fitted with specialized cameras have begun mapping the mineral composition of the Moon.

this is another example of the influence that Earth and Moon have on one another.

A double planet

The Moon is so large compared to the Earth that some astronomers believe they should really be considered a "double

planet." The Moon's most obvious effect on our planet is in the daily rise and fall of Earth's oceans—the tides. The Moon's gravity pulls the oceans toward it, creating a bulge in the seas on both sides of our planet. As Earth spins on its axis, these bulges move around the planet, so every part of the planet experiences

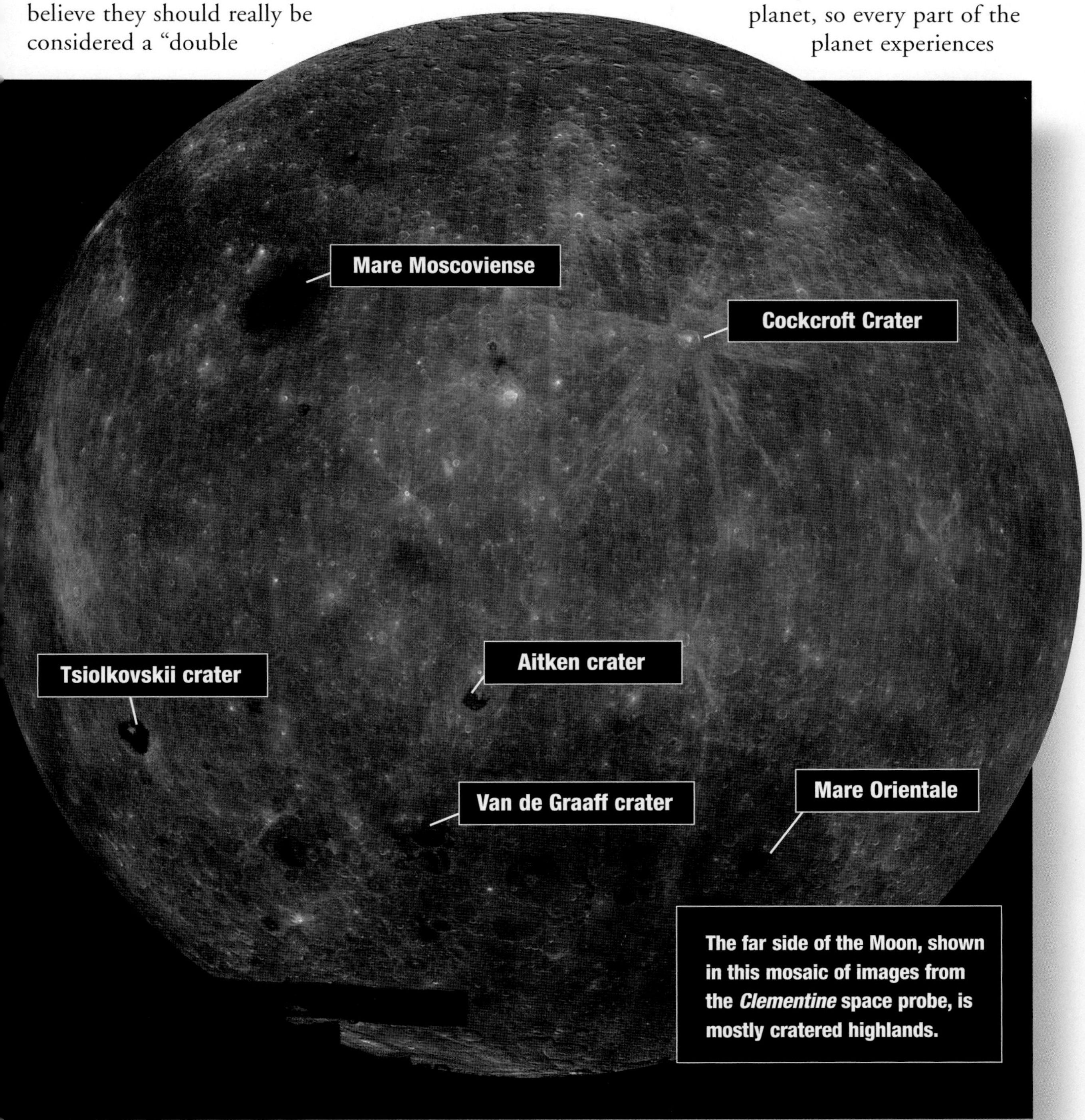

Mare Moscoviense

Cockcroft Crater

Tsiolkovskii crater

Aitken crater

Van de Graaff crater

Mare Orientale

The far side of the Moon, shown in this mosaic of images from the *Clementine* space probe, is mostly cratered highlands.

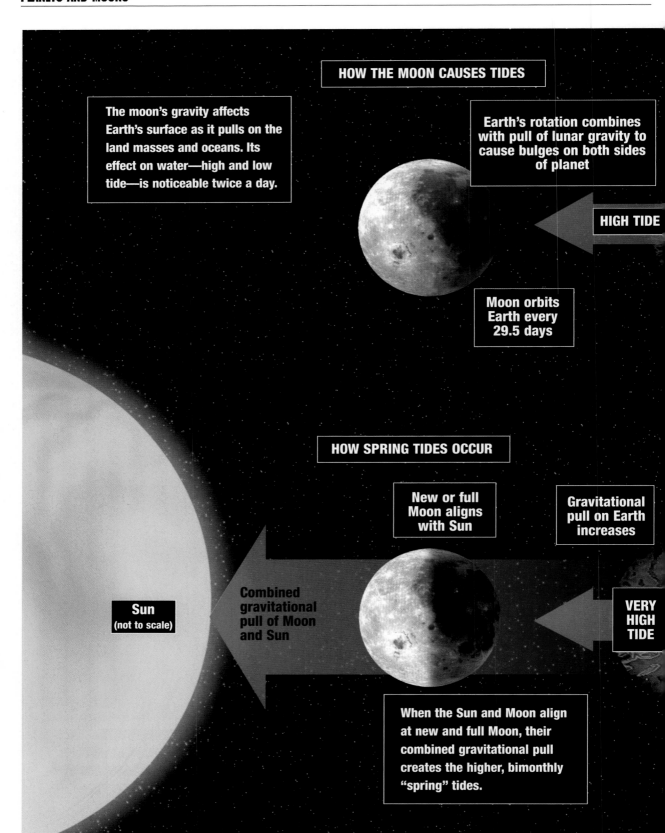

HOW THE MOON CAUSES TIDES

The moon's gravity affects Earth's surface as it pulls on the land masses and oceans. Its effect on water—high and low tide—is noticeable twice a day.

Earth's rotation combines with pull of lunar gravity to cause bulges on both sides of planet

HIGH TIDE

Moon orbits Earth every 29.5 days

HOW SPRING TIDES OCCUR

New or full Moon aligns with Sun

Gravitational pull on Earth increases

Sun
(not to scale)

Combined gravitational pull of Moon and Sun

VERY HIGH TIDE

When the Sun and Moon align at new and full Moon, their combined gravitational pull creates the higher, bimonthly "spring" tides.

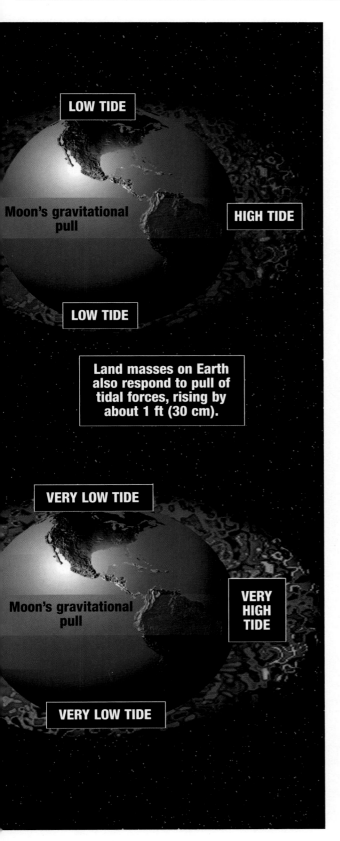

LOW TIDE

Moon's gravitational pull

HIGH TIDE

LOW TIDE

Land masses on Earth also respond to pull of tidal forces, rising by about 1 ft (30 cm).

VERY LOW TIDE

Moon's gravitational pull

VERY HIGH TIDE

VERY LOW TIDE

high and low tides twice a day. The Sun's gravity has a similar but weaker effect, and depending on the directions of Sun and Moon, it counterbalances, or reinforces, the lunar tides. When Moon and Sun pull in the same or opposite directions, high "spring" tides result. When they pull at right angles to each other, the result is low "neap" tides.

Tidal forces don't just affect Earth's oceans, of course—our planet's liquid layer just makes the effect more noticeable. Earth's crust also flexes, rising gently by about 1 foot (30 cm) with the tides. Earth's gravity has a similar effect on the Moon. In the Moon's case, as with many of the planet's satellites, tidal forces have caused its rotation to slow until it matches its orbit (a so-called "synchronous" rotation). The Moon's orbit has also spiraled outward, and it continues to move away from Earth by about 1.6 inches (4 cm) each year. The Moon's tidal pull has a similar effect on Earth, and our own planet's rotation is gradually slowing down: 300 million years ago, a day was just twenty-one hours long.

Earth's gravity can also explain the difference between the surface of the Moon's near and far sides. In ancient times, when the Moon was still partially molten, Earth's gravity tugged the inner molten layers toward itself. The heavier, molten material moved slightly closer to the lunar surface on the Earth-facing side. Lava eruptions that created the maria thus found it easier to reach the surface on the near side, while only the deepest basins on the far side flooded.

The Moon may have an important role in protecting Earth and making it suitable for life. Some astronomers speculate that the Moon has "soaked up" meteor impacts that might otherwise have struck Earth, and its tidal pull may also have helped keep Earth's axis of rotation steady throughout its history. Without this, the axis of Earth's spin might have begun wobbling back and forth, creating dramatic changes in climate similar to those seen on Mars.

CHAPTER 3

EXTREME ENVIRONMENTS

Mercury, Venus, and Mars, the three other planets of the inner solar system, all have certain similarities to Earth. They all formed from the same part of the solar nebula and are rocky worlds of roughly similar size. But they have developed into radically different worlds, each with unique characteristics.

Mercury

Mercury, the innermost planet, at just 3,029 miles (4,875 km) across, is the second smallest after Pluto. Only one space probe has visited it so far, and we know surprisingly little about it. Images sent back by *Mariner 10* revealed an airless, cratered world that at first glance seems similar to the Moon.

Mercury's day lasts about 59 Earth days. It spins three times on its axis for every two orbits around the Sun. (Like Moon's synchronous rotation around Earth, this arrangement keeps tidal forces to a minimum). When the planet is closest to the Sun, and traveling fastest in its orbit, the Sun's movement across its sky can actually be reversed—some parts of Mercury experience two sunrises in one day! Mercury's size and closeness to the Sun mean that it cannot hold onto a dense atmosphere, so the surface is alternately baked and frozen through the long days and nights. In the course of a single day, temperatures can vary from −280 to 800 °F (−170 to 430 °C).

Mercury's surface is heavily cratered. Some of the larger craters or impact basins are filled with "seas" of solidified lava similar to those on the Moon. The largest feature is the huge Caloris Basin, which is a crater 840 miles (1,340 km) across, ringed by huge chains of mountains. The impact that formed the basin was so violent that it sent shockwaves all the way around the planet. A jumbled landscape, called "chaotic terrain," marks the region where the shockwaves met on the other side.

Shortly after landing on Mars in January 2004, NASA's *Mars Spirit Rover* sent back this spectacular high-resolution image of the dusty, rock-strewn surface.

Mercury's most distinctive features are the huge cliffs that run across its surface. These cliffs probably formed as sections of the ground slipped past each other sometime after the main crater formed. In some cases, the two sides of a crater differ in height by several miles (km).

What could have formed these cliffs? It seems that at some point in its history, after most of the craters formed on its surface, Mercury's interior heated up and expanded, cracking the crust in places before shrinking again. Some of the cracked segments of crust then slipped down past the others to fill in the gaps, creating the cliffs in the process.

This strange period of heating and expansion may be linked to the fact that Mercury has a much bigger core than any of the other terrestrial planets, as revealed by measurements of its density. The most likely explanation for this is that Mercury was struck by a rogue planetoid early in its history, and that the impact carried away much of the planet's original crust and mantle.

Venus

Venus is Earth's nonidentical twin. With a diameter of 7,521 miles (12,104 km), and orbiting just 26 million miles (42 million km) closer to the Sun than Earth, we might expect

This mosaic of photos from *Mariner 10,* the only space probe to reach Mercury so far, shows a cratered, moonlike world.

Venus to be more like our planet. Instead, it has a dense, choking atmosphere, corrosive acid rains, and searing surface temperatures of about 870 °F (470 °C). Venus also has a bizarre "day." It rotates in the opposite direction of all the other planets and turns around on its axis once every 243 Earth days. Its sunlit "day" lasts 117 Earth days, and it makes one trip all the way around the Sun in about 225 Earth days. In other words, one day and night on Venus (243 days) lasts longer than its entire year (225 days)!

Venus's atmosphere is dominated by carbon dioxide, and clouds of sulfuric acid completely hide its surface from view. From space, Venus looks like a featureless, yellow-white ball. Space probes have mapped the surface from orbit using radar to peer through the clouds, and a few

heavily shielded robotic landing vehicles have survived long enough to send back surface pictures to Earth.

These studies reveal that Venus's surface is remarkably young. In spite of its heavy atmosphere, we would expect more impact craters on the surface, but there are only a few. Geologists think this indicates that nearly the entire surface of Venus was wiped clean by massive volcanic eruptions about half a billion years ago.

Volcanoes are the dominant feature of the landscape of Venus. They are found everywhere,

The main image below, taken by _Pioneer Venus Orbiter_ in 1979, shows Venus permanently cloaked in a choking atmosphere. The smaller photos show its sequence of phases as seen from Earth.

in a wide variety of shapes and sizes. No one knows for certain whether there are active volcanoes on Venus today, but some probes detected lightning during their descent through the atmosphere, and active volcanoes on Earth are often associated with lightning. Radar maps show a surface covered with smooth lava flows and cracked areas of solidified lava.

The widespread volcanic resurfacing of Venus may be a regular event, and may be connected with the lack of tectonic plates on the planet. On Earth, tectonic plates allow volcanic material to escape along the joints between plates, releasing heat from the planet's interior. With no tectonic plates to allow heat to escape, the interior of Venus is like a giant pressure cooker. When the temperature and pressure become high enough, molten material forces its way to the surface all over the planet.

Mars

Unmistakable thanks to its rusty red color, Mars has fascinated astronomers for centuries. Despite its relatively small diameter of 4,213 miles (6,780 km), and position farther from the Sun, Mars is the planet most like Earth. Each new robot space probe uncovers new parallels between the two worlds.

The martian landscape shows a wide range of features. Cratered highlands similar to those seen on the Moon dominate the southern hemisphere, while the northern hemisphere has smooth plains and a number of towering volcanoes. The largest of these sit on top of the Tharsis Bulge, a huge bulge in the planet's surface, 6 miles (10 km) high and 2,500 miles (4,000 km) across. Olympus Mons, the largest volcano in the solar system, rises to 17 miles (27 km) high. By counting the number of

COMPARING THE TERRESTRIAL PLANETS

Many of the differences between the four terrestrial planets can be explained by two factors—their different sizes and their positions in the solar system. The collisions that created the planets would have released a lot of excess energy as heat, but the smaller planets would have built up less of this heat, and have also lost it more rapidly. So, while Earth (and perhaps Venus) still have molten cores, Mercury's core froze solid long ago. Astronomers believe the core of Mars, which once drove volcanic activity, has solidified by now. The heat from a molten core still drives volcanic activity on Venus and Earth.

But why are the types of activity so different? Only Earth has drifting tectonic plates, although Venus has some signs that plates began to form in its distant past. The lack of plates could simply be connected to the size of the planets (it almost certainly explains why there are no plates on Mars and Mercury) but the best explanation could have something to do with the lack of water on Venus. On Earth, the water cycle creates carbonate rocks that are lighter than the basalt rocks formed in volcanic eruptions. The existence of rocks with different densities means that, where plates collide, one rock is more likely to be forced under the other, to melt, and then be recycled in

impact craters on different parts of the martian surface, and comparing them to the lack of craters on some of the volcanic lava flows, astronomers have determined that the volcanoes were probably active as recently as 150 million years ago. This is not very long in geological terms, and means that some volcanoes could still be active today.

Along the south side of the Tharsis Rise runs a gigantic canyon, the Valles Marineris, which was probably caused by the crust buckling under the weight of the bulge. The Valles Marineris is named after Mariner 9, the space probe that

This photo of Mars clearly shows the vast scar of the Valles Marineris, a huge geological fault caused by the rising of the Tharsis Bulge to its north.

Subduction: Where plates of different densities meet on Earth, the lighter one is forced downward into the mantle, melting as it does so. The heavier one may buckle upward, forming a mountain range.

Crust creation: Where two plates move apart, material from the mantle comes to the surface, creating a chain of volcanoes (usually underwater).

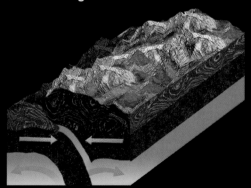

the Earth's upper mantle. This process, called "subduction" prevents a rocky traffic jam from building up inside the Earth, keeps the plates moving around,

and stops pressure and heat from building up. This is something that could not happen on Venus, where all the rocks are of similar density.

discovered it. It is long enough to cut across the continent of North America, and at 6 miles (10 km) deep in places, it dwarfs Earth's Grand Canyon, which is only one mile (1.6 km) deep and 180 miles (290 km) long.

With a rotation period of about 25 hours, and an axis tilted at 25 degrees from vertical, Mars experiences days and seasons remarkably like those of Earth. It also has icy polar caps, though these are far smaller and thinner than the polar ice on Earth. The southern cap is mostly made of carbon dioxide ice, which turns directly into a gas below the freezing point of water. As a result, this cap comes and goes as its carbon dioxide evaporates into the atmosphere in the spring and forms again over the permafrost (ice mixed with soil) during the fall. Mars's northern polar cap is more substantial, because the carbon dioxide sits on top of a layer of actual water ice.

The atmosphere of Mars is thin, with just one percent of Earth's atmospheric pressure. It is dominated by carbon dioxide, and does not act as a very good insulator. As a result, temperatures on Mars can vary between 80 °F (30 °C) at noon, and –210 °F (–130 °C) at midnight. Clouds, mostly of water and carbon dioxide ice, regularly form in the martian atmosphere, but the most impressive martian weather systems are the great dust storms that occasionally engulf parts of the planet. When Mars is closest to the Sun and there is more energy to power these storms, the planet's entire surface can be hidden from the Sun for several months. Fine red dust is everywhere on Mars. The red color comes from iron oxide (rust), which tints the martian skies a pale pink in photographs taken from the surface.

Mars is the only other planet that was probably shaped by running water. Billions of years ago, oceans likely covered large parts of its surface, and rivers cut distinctive channels across the landscape. Climate change in the distant past meant that most of the water disappeared from Mars's surface. Some of the water evaporated into space, but probes indicate that large amounts sank below

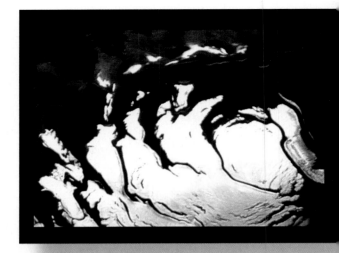

Above: Seasonal temperature changes cause the carbon dioxide in the martian polar caps to evaporate and later recondense, giving the caps a beautiful, layered appearance.

Below: A computer-generated image of Olympus Mons emphasizes its height of 17 miles (27 km). Its diameter stretches for hundreds of miles (km).

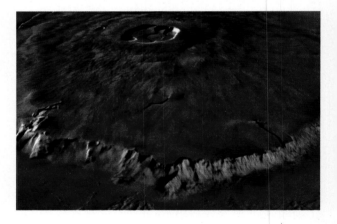

the landscape to form a far-reaching subsurface layer of permafrost, especially in the southern hemisphere. Other data indicates that water could have emerged onto the martian surface from time to time. Some hillsides and other slopes show distinctive gullies where water appears to have burst out from underground and washed a stream of debris downhill. The lack of craters in some of these areas suggests that the gullies are very recent, and that such processes still occur.

LIFE ON MARS?

Mars has always been seen as the most likely planet in the solar system to support life, and while advanced creatures, such as animals, can now be ruled out, it is highly possible that simple life forms had begun to evolve when the planet's surface was still wet. In 1996, a team of NASA scientists analyzing a meteorite known as ALH84001, which had been blasted off Mars millions of years ago, discovered possible traces of life in the form of certain chemicals and perhaps even "microfossils" of tiny creatures similar to bacteria. If life did begin sometime during the ancient history of Mars, it could still be there today—adapted to the extreme conditions of the surface or hidden below the surface.

THE CANALS OF MARS

In 1877, Italian astronomer Giovanni Schiaparelli (1835–1910) noticed straight lines apparently joining many of the darker areas of Mars's surface. When he reported them, Schiaparelli used an Italian term, *canali* (meaning simply channels). People misinterpreted his report as the possibility of the existence of intelligent Martians. Someone even suggested that the "canals" formed part of an irrigation system that carried water from the polar ice caps to the drier regions around the equator. The main problem with this theory was that while some reported seeing the canals clearly, others did not see them at all. A few astronomers recognized right away that the canals were simply an optical illusion. It took many decades for others to believe the truth.

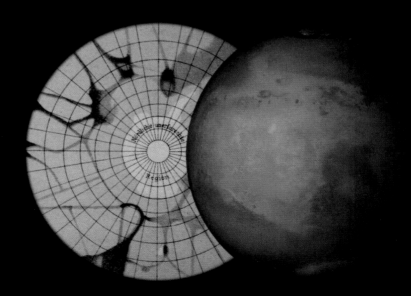

Comparing one of Schiaparelli's original maps of the *canali* to a modern photograph of the Red Planet reveals the truth: The *canali* were nothing more than an optical illusion.

AMONG THE GIANTS

Beyond the asteroid belt lies the realm of the giant planets. Huge balls of gas, liquid, and slushy ice, these giants have only small cores of rock at their centers. Large families of satellites orbit each of these enormous worlds, and some of those moons are fascinating and active places themselves.

Jupiter

Jupiter, the king of the planets, is almost twelve times the size of Earth, with a diameter of 88,846 miles (142,984 km). It is a huge ball of mostly hydrogen gas. Small amounts of other chemicals, often based on sulfur, make up Jupiter as well, and these cause its upper layers to be extremely colorful. In normal conditions, hydrogen gas consists of two atoms of hydrogen (indicated by the symbol H_2) joined together, which forms a stable molecule. Inside a gas giant such as Jupiter, however, the pressure becomes

so great that the hydrogen is compressed to form a liquid layer. Then—deeper still—the hydrogen is broken apart into atoms, forming a liquid that behaves like a metal. (No one knows for sure, but many astronomers believe Jupiter's rocky core center is roughly Earth-sized.)

Jupiter is also contracting slowly under the pull of its own gravity. As a result, it generates heat internally. Along with radiation from the Sun, this heat helps drive the storms in Jupiter's upper atmosphere.

Jupiter's weather, like Earth's, consists of areas of high and low pressure areas. The high-pressure areas create clearings in the upper atmosphere, revealing cloud layers at greater depth and with different colors. But because Jupiter spins once every ten hours (fast enough to cause a noticeable bulge around the planet's equator), the weather systems have become stretched out into bands that

Gas giant Jupiter is so huge and spins so rapidly that it bulges noticeably outward at the equator. The rapid spin, with heat generated deep inside, drives the planet's complex and powerful weather systems.

31

wrap all the way around the planet. This gives Jupiter its distinctive striped appearance.

One exception to the striped belts and zones of Jupiter's atmosphere is the Great Red Spot. This enormous, slowly circling storm is large enough to swallow several Earths. It is an area of very low pressure, and astronomers have been able to see it for at least three centuries.

The swirling layer of liquid, metallic hydrogen deep inside Jupiter generates a powerful magnetic field that surrounds the planet. Blown out into space by the "solar wind," Jupiter's magnetic field stretches as far as Saturn's orbit.

At least sixty satellites orbit Jupiter. Some formed from the same cloud of material as the planet itself, while others are asteroids captured later by Jupiter's enormously powerful gravity. The largest and most impressive are the Galilean moons, discovered by Galileo Galilei in 1610.

Io, the innermost Galilean moon, is a red, yellow, and black moon, pockmarked by the constant eruptions of sulfur volcanoes on its surface. It is at the mercy of Jupiter's powerful gravitational tidal forces, and these forces heat up Io's interior, making Io the most volcanic body in the solar system.

Europa is a world of ice, with a smooth white surface crisscrossed by multicolored lines. The lines are thought to be the healed scars of past cracks in the icy crust. There is strong evidence that Europa's visible surface is in fact a vast ice sheet floating on a deep ocean of liquid water, kept warm by tidal heating of its core.

Ganymede is the largest moon in the entire solar system, and is bigger than both Mercury and Pluto. Its surface seems to consist of old, bright regions, set in a darker, more recent surface. One theory is that tidal forces broke up

An artist's impression of Jupiter rising above the mottled surface of Ganymede, based on images returned by *Voyager 2*.

Ganymede's surface seems to have broken apart and refrozen in fresh icy slush.

Dark areas indicate fresh new material.

Light areas indicate older material.

the old surface and submerged it in a slushy layer of ice, which later refroze.

Callisto, the most distant of the Galilean moons, has a dark surface pitted by brilliant icy craters. Its most mysterious feature is its magnetic field, which seems to be generated by an ocean of salty water underneath the crust.

Saturn

Most famous for its rings, Saturn itself is a yellowish-white ball of gas, similar in composition and structure to Jupiter. It looks different because, lying farther away from the Sun, the upper layers of its atmosphere are colder. This allows clouds of ammonia crystals to form around Saturn, obscuring much of the detail below. Despite this, the planet's bands can still be made out, along with occasional "white spots." (These are smaller, short-lived versions of Jupiter's Great Red Spot.) Saturn is the least-dense planet: If placed in water, it would float!

Even though all the gas giant planets have rings, none can rival Saturn's rings. While their outer limits extend to almost 300,000 miles (480,000 km) from the planet, they are less than 1 mile (1.6 km) deep. These great disks of material puzzled early astronomers. It was not until the nineteenth century that Scottish physicist James Clerk Maxwell (1831–1879) explained that countless small objects must

form them, each following its own orbit around the planet. The rings are directly above Saturn's equator, but because Saturn's axis is tilted at almost 27 degrees, we see different views of the rings during each of Saturn's years. Every fifteen Earth years, the angle of the rings makes them disappear completely from our view.

Two main rings, the A and B rings, are brightest, and separated by a distinct dark gap, named the Cassini Division, after its discoverer, astronomer Giovanni Cassini (1625-1712). Numerous other rings, most of which are very fine, encircle Saturn. Some of the rings contain "shepherd moons" whose own gravity keeps the ring particles in orbit. In all, hundreds of thousands of rings may orbit Saturn.

As might be expected, Saturn has a huge family of moons. Many are small and probably help refresh the rings with new material. Others are captured asteroids. Still more of the moons form unique and interesting worlds of their own. Mimas, the closest of these to Saturn, bears the scar of an enormous impact crater. Enceladus is a tiny but active moon with a brilliant white surface, apparently kept fresh by eruptions of snowy ice from below.

Tethys, Dione, and Rhea are larger worlds of rock and ice, too far away to be heated by Saturn's tidal forces. Tethys and Rhea show signs that they were once like Enceladus, but erupted ice from the interior covers many of their craters. Iapetus has a bizarre surface, half bright and half dark. The dark half may be coated with material somehow produced by the outermost large moon—the captured asteroid Phoebe.

Between Rhea and Iapetus sits Titan, the largest of Saturn's satellites, and a world only slightly smaller than Ganymede. It is the only

Saturn looms through the hazy orange atmosphere of Titan in this artist's impression. The successful landing of the *Huygens* probe in early 2005 has confirmed that this picture is a reasonably accurate impression of Titan's surface.

E-Ring

A-Ring

B-Ring

Cassini Division

Saturn

C- or Crepe Ring

PLANETARY RINGS

The ring systems of the four giant planets are all very different from one another. They range from the magnificent rings of Saturn, composed of large icy boulders, through the dark and dusty rings of Uranus and the degraded rings of Neptune, to the faint sheet of dust around Jupiter.

The best explanation for all these types of rings is that they are phases in the history of a short-lived phenomenon.

Most astronomers think that rings form when a small object (a comet, asteroid, or moonlet) is broken up by a planet's gravity. Collisions between the fragments gradually grind them down and spread them out in orbit around the planet's equator. As the ring particles gradually sift down into the planet's atmosphere, they burn up, and the rings fade away. Of course, the size and type of object that originally formed the rings has a big

Saturn's rings have a very complex structure, with thousands of individual ringlets. This diagram shows some of the main elements, as mapped through Earth-based telescopes.

moon in the solar system with a substantial atmosphere. This is dominated by nitrogen but includes enough methane to create an impenetrable orange haze around it. The Cassini space probe to Saturn, equipped to peer through the haze and place a robot lander on the surface, revealed a fascinating world in which methane seems to have the same role as water on Earth. The methane exists in three states—liquid, solid, and vapor—and has carved out features that look eerily like Earth's rivers and lakes. Some astronomers and biologists think that Titan's atmosphere resembles that of prehistoric Earth, and that life might one day evolve there.

Uranus and Neptune

The outer gas giants, Uranus and Neptune, are very similar to each other, but very different from gas giants Jupiter and Saturn. Both have diameters about four times the size of Earth, and both are bluish-green in color, although Uranus is slightly greener and Neptune is slightly bluer.

These two planets are often called "ice giants," because they formed the area of the young solar system that was rich in chemical ices that melt relatively easily. These planets are mainly composed of such ices. Each probably has a rocky core about the size of Earth, surrounded by a slushy icy mantle. An atmosphere of hydrogen and helium surrounds the mantle.

Neptune, like Jupiter and Saturn, has obvious weather systems—including the strongest winds in the solar system—powered largely by heat from its interior.

Uranus, is the odd one out among the ice giants because it does not seem to have an internal power source. In fact, Uranus appeared almost featureless when the *Voyager 2* space probe flew past it in 1986.

This lack of activity could be linked to Uranus's most unusual feature, which is its axis of rotation. Instead of being upright or slightly tilted from the vertical, Uranus's axis is knocked over at an angle of 98 degrees from vertical. This means it rolls on its side as it orbits the Sun. This gives the planet very unusual seasons during its orbit, which takes 84 Earth years. The poles experience a day and night cycle that takes forty-two years,

influence on their appearance. According to this theory, Saturn's rings must have formed from a large icy comet breaking up in the recent past, while Uranus's system might have been created from a smaller and darker object during a much earlier time span.

These "bruises" on Jupiter were caused by a comet impact in 1994. If the comet had broken up in orbit around Jupiter, it might have formed a new ring system.

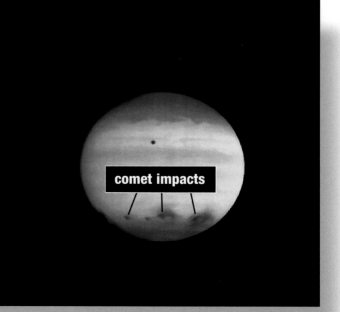

comet impacts

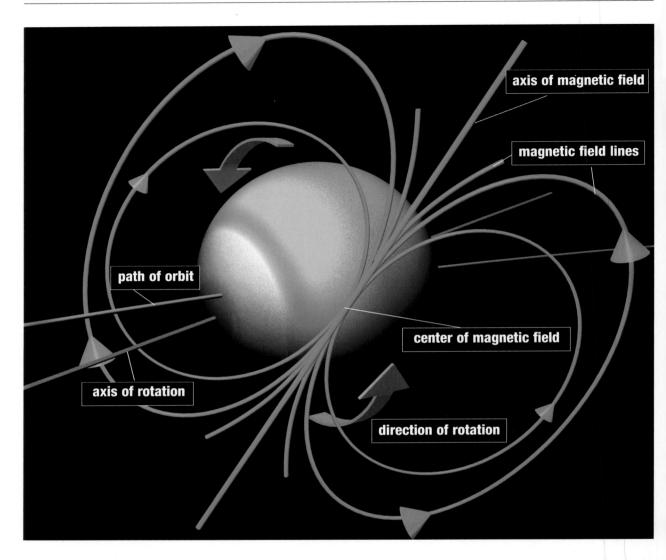

axis of magnetic field

magnetic field lines

path of orbit

center of magnetic field

axis of rotation

direction of rotation

Uranus's axis of rotation and equator are tipped 98 degrees from vertical. Uranus's magnetic field has a peculiar alignment that does not even pass through the center of the planet.

while the equator has a seventeen-hour day. It is likely that the huge differences in temperature between parts of Uranus churn up the atmosphere so much that normal weather systems cannot form, at least during part of the planet's orbit.

What knocked Uranus off its axis? The most likely explanation is an interplanetary collision occurred sometime in its past. The magnetic fields of the ice giants, on the other hand, are

more difficult to explain. They are at wild angles to the axis of rotation, and in the case of Uranus, the axis of the magnetic field does not even pass through the center of the planet. Magnetic fields in the ice giants are probably created in the mantle instead of the core, which is different from terrestrial planets' magnetic field origins.

Uranus has a substantial system of rings that are narrow and dark compared to the rings around Saturn. It also has a number of moons, including five substantial ones—Miranda, Ariel, Umbriel, Titania, and Oberon. Neptune also has a handful of faint rings, but its moon system is unusual, dominated by a huge icy world called Triton. This moon orbits in the opposite direction to Neptune's own rotation, suggesting that it did not form alongside Neptune, but was captured later, flinging Neptune's natural moons into wildly eccentric orbits or ejecting them from the system altogether. Triton itself is a fascinating world, with geysers of ice erupting slushy material onto the surface at temperatures of about −390 °F (−235 °C). Many astronomers think Triton is a captured "ice dwarf" from the Kuiper Belt. If they are right, then pictures of Triton offer our first glimpse of a world similar to Pluto.

WILLIAM HERSCHEL

German-born William Herschel (1738–1822) was a professional musician who moved to England in 1757 and started building telescopes as part of his astronomy hobby. In 1781, while surveying the sky for nebulae, he discovered Uranus. At first, he thought the new object was a comet. When he calculated its orbit, he realized he had discovered a new planet. The discovery made Herschel famous and led to his appointment as the King's astronomer. His sister and son also made important astronomical discoveries.

THE DISCOVERY OF NEPTUNE

Neptune was the first planet to be discovered through calculation rather than observation. Astronomers had constant problems predicting the position of Uranus after its discovery in 1781, and it became clear that something else was affecting its orbit. Two mathematicians, British John Couch Adams (1819–1892) and French Urbain LeVerrier (1811–1877) independently calculated the position of a new planet beyond Uranus. Adams could not get anyone to take his theory seriously. In 1846, however, LeVerrier contacted Johann Galle of the Berlin Observatory, and Galle located the new planet immediately.

The Sun is little more than a brilliant star as seen through the tenuous rings of distant Neptune. The eighth planet somehow generates enough internal heat to drive some of the strongest winds in the solar system.

CHAPTER 5

MINOR WORLDS

Between and beyond the major planets of the solar system, countless smaller objects orbit the Sun. They range from tiny dust particles to worlds hundreds of miles across. In general, the rocky bodies that orbit relatively close to the Sun are called asteroids, while the icy ones that spend most of their orbits far from the Sun are called comets. The division between the two is not clear-cut, however. Recent years have also seen the discovery of a new class of objects, sometimes called "ice dwarfs," orbiting beyond Neptune.

Pluto and Charon

Pluto is usually counted as the ninth planet. American astronomer Clyde Tombaugh (1906–1997) discovered it in 1930, during a deliberate search for a planet that could be affecting Neptune's orbit. The fact that Pluto happened to be in the right position at the time was a coincidence. Astronomers soon realized

that it was far too small to be affecting its giant neighbor. In 2005, astronomers finally announced the discovery (in 2003) of what could be a tenth planet, which is not yet named. (*See page 42.*)

Pluto is the smallest planet, with a diameter of just 1,430 miles (2,300 km)—considerably smaller than Mercury. It also has a wild orbit that tilts at 17 degrees to the plane of the solar system and most of the other planets. Pluto's orbit is so elliptical that it spends twenty years of every 249-year orbit nearer the Sun than Neptune. At first, there was speculation that Pluto might be a lost satellite of Neptune, but we now know that the two planets are in orbits that always keep them far away from each other.

Because our space probes have not yet visited Pluto, we know little about it. Studying its light has revealed that it has a thin atmosphere and is coated with frozen carbon monoxide, nitrogen, and methane

Charon hangs above the surface of Pluto in this artist's impression. Both worlds are covered in a mixture of chemical ices. When they are closest to the Sun, some of Pluto's ice evaporates to form a thin atmosphere.

ices. It probably resembles Neptune's giant satellite Triton, because the two worlds are both thought to be members of the Kuiper Belt (*see page 41*).

Pluto's giant moon Charon was discovered in 1978, when American astronomer James Christy (b. 1938) noticed a "bump" in the side of the planet on high-resolution photos. Many times larger than our own Moon, Charon is about half Pluto's size, and orbits just 12,000 miles (19,400 km) from Pluto. The system is a true "double planet," because the tidal forces between planet and moon have slowed both down into synchronous rotation—Pluto and Charon both rotate in 6.4 days, the same time Charon takes to go around Pluto. From one side of Pluto, Charon hangs permanently in the sky, but from the other side, it is never seen at all.

Asteroids

Between the orbits of Mars and Jupiter, at roughly 158 to 372 million miles (254 to 598 million km) from the Sun, lies a zone filled with smaller, rocky worlds. These asteroids, ranging in size from Ceres, 580 miles (930 km) across, to boulders of a few yards or less, were once thought to be the debris from a destroyed planet. Today, however, we know that they represent material that never formed a planet in the first

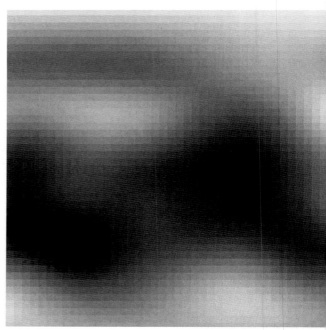

place, but found a stable niche between the inner and outer solar systems.

The main asteroid belt is probably home to about ten billion substantial asteroids, but it covers such a huge region that most of the asteroids are well spaced out. Asteroids are not confined to this region. Two groups called "Trojans" share Jupiter's orbit, moving far enough ahead and behind it to avoid its gravity, and many Near-Earth Asteroids (NEAs) travel through the

THE CELESTIAL POLICE

In the late 1700s, after the discovery of Uranus, many astronomers were fascinated by a mathematical rule called the Titius-Bode Law, which seemed to correctly predict the positions of the planets. The only problem was a gap in the sequence between Mars and Jupiter. A small group, organized by Hungarian Franz Xavier von Zach of the Seeberg Observatory in Germany, that called

itself the "celestial police" agreed to collaborate in a search for the missing planet. But Sicilian astronomer Giuseppe Piazzi, who discovered Ceres on New Year's Day, 1801, beat them to the first discovery. They helped Piazzi relocate the asteroid later in the year, after it was lost as it passed behind the Sun. Convinced that Ceres was too small to be their missing planet, the celestial police continued their search. They discovered

inner solar system in stretched elliptical orbits.

These NEAs are the most-studied asteroids because they present a possible threat to Earth. They seem to have originated in the main asteroid belt and were probably expelled after straying into one of the "Kirkwood gaps." These gaps are relatively empty regions of the asteroid belt affected by Jupiter's gravity, which eventually flings asteroids into different orbits.

Pluto is too far away to map directly, but thanks to its moon, we now have a basic idea of its surface colors and brightness. Between 1985 and 1991, Charon and Pluto happened to align with Earth so that they passed in front of each other and created a series of eclipses. By measuring the changes in light when one world blocked the other, astronomers were able to figure out the brightness of different regions on the surface of both worlds.

The Kuiper Belt

In 1992, astronomers using the Hubble Space Telescope detected a new object moving in the space beyond Neptune. It was the first evidence for a theoretical "doughnut" of icy worlds around Pluto. This area is usually known as the Kuiper Belt, named after the Dutch-American space scientist Gerard Kuiper (1905–1973), who first suggested its existence. Since then, many new Kuiper Belt Objects (KBOs) have been discovered.

The KBOs are thought to be "ice dwarfs"— the outer solar system's equivalent of the asteroids nearer the Sun. The largest are about the size of Pluto or bigger, but the smallest are probably no more than a few miles across. Many comets pass

Pallas in 1802, Juno in 1804, and Vesta in 1807. As more and more of these new objects were found, John Herschel (1792–1871), the son of William Herschel, discoverer of Uranus, suggested that these objects should be called asteroids, which means "starlike objects."

An artist's impression of the largest asteroid, Ceres. In the distance, another asteroid is silhouetted against the Sun.

through the Kuiper Belt at their farthest point from the Sun, suggesting that they start their lives here and are knocked into new orbits by collisions with each other or close encounters with Neptune.

Several KBOs have been announced as "tenth planets" by their discoverers, but the first real candidate for this title is 2003UB313, a KBO that is definitely larger than Pluto. It is at least 1,670 miles (2,700 km) across. The discovery of this KBO brings Pluto's own status into question. Astronomers are still arguing over whether or not to officially consider 2003UB313 the tenth planet. If that happens, astronomers would have to add new "planets" every time a KBO bigger than Pluto is discovered.

The Kuiper Belt probably dissipates at about 10 billion miles (16 billion km) from the Sun. Beyond this distance, the solar nebula was too thin to form even ice dwarfs. Still, ice dwarfs are not the most distant objects in the solar system. Even further out, we find the Oort Cloud (*see box, page 43*). There is also a mysterious red object called Sedna, discovered in 2003, that orbits between the Kuiper Belt and Oort Cloud. This is probably an asteroid that was flung into a new orbit by an encounter with Jupiter.

An artist's impression of the Kuiper Belt—though in reality it is not this crowded.

THE OORT CLOUD

The Oort Cloud is a huge spherical shell of comets that surrounds the solar system. Its existence was first proposed by Dutch astronomer Jan Oort (1900–1992), who realized that it was the only way of explaining the "long-period" comets that arrive from the depths of the Solar System. These icy visitors can approach from any angle. Their maximum distances from the Sun average about one light-year (6 trillion miles or 10 trillion km).

The comets in the Oort Cloud probably did not form in that location. They more likely formed around the region where Uranus and Neptune currently orbit and were flung into their present orbits by the gravity of these giant planets. Some astronomers believe passing stars occasionally disrupt the Oort Cloud and send large numbers of comets plunging into the inner solar system, where they could potentially bombard the planets and cause extinctions on Earth.

The Oort Cloud surrounds our solar system like a cocoon. When disturbed, long-period comets from the Oort Cloud may enter the inner solar system from any direction. Long-period comets have orbits so large that they pass through the inner solar system only once.

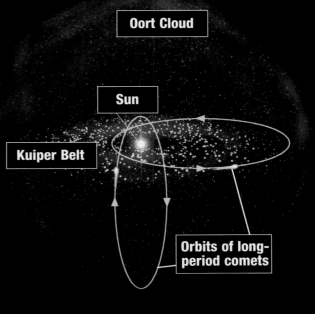

Oort Cloud

Sun

Kuiper Belt

Orbits of long-period comets

Comets

Comets are icy objects from the outer solar system. Usually a few miles across, they inhabit the regions of the Kuiper Belt and the much more distant Oort Cloud (*see above*). They only become visible from Earth when they fall into elliptical orbits that bring them much closer to the Sun at one end. As a comet falls toward the inner solar system, its surface is heated by the Sun. Comet "crusts" are often coated with very dark "organic" (carbon-based) chemicals, and this makes them very good absorbers of heat.

As the ice below the crust heats up and evaporates, jets of water and dust burst out through the surface, and the comet develops a huge cloud around it, called the coma. Some material blasted out by the comet is blown away from the Sun by the solar wind, and may form one or more tails. The tail always points away from the Sun, so it follows the coma and central nucleus of the comet as they approach the inner solar system. The tail leads the way back to the outer regions once the comet has swung past perihelion (its closest point to the Sun).

Comets fall into two groups: short-period comets that orbit the Sun in less than two hundred years, and long-period comets which orbit in many thousands of years. Long-period comets originate in the Oort Cloud and may appear without warning. Most bright comets have long periods. They are very unpredictable, however, and a comet that looks bright when discovered in the outer solar system may not live up to expectations.

Short-period comets probably originate in the Kuiper Belt. They may also have begun as long-period comets whose distant orbits were

When the European *Giotto* probe flew through Halley's Comet in 1986, it produced this spectacular view of the comet's peanut-shaped nucleus.

disturbed by a close encounter with the gravitational field of one of the giant planets. The shortest-period comet known is the very faint Comet Encke, which orbits the Sun in just 3.3 years. The brightest and most famous short-period comet is Halley's Comet. It returns every seventy-six years and has been recorded throughout human history. Every time a comet passes the Sun, it burns away a little more of its

COMETS, WATER, AND LIFE

With their huge quantities of ice water and plentiful organic chemicals, comets could have played a vital role in the development of life on Earth. When the terrestrial planets formed, temperatures close to the Sun would have been too hot for ice to survive in the solar nebula. As a result, all the planets would have been dry. But at some point in their histories, Venus, Earth, and Mars all had substantial oceans—so where did they come from? One popular theory is that the oceans were created as comets bombarded the inner planets. Some astronomers say this is still happening, and that millions of tons of water arrive in Earth's atmosphere daily as smaller chunks of ice from space evaporate. Others suggest that comets carried organic chemicals, or even living organisms, to Earth in the first place.

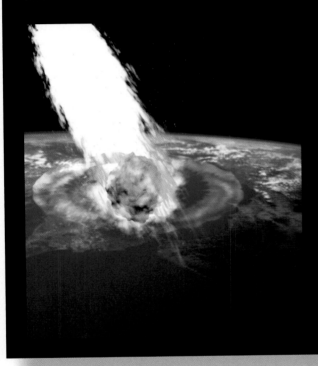

An artist's impression of a huge comet crashing to Earth. Such impacts may have brought vast quantities of water to Earth. They could also be a threat to life, causing mass-extinction events such as the one that killed the dinosaurs.

reservoir of ice, so short-period comets have a limited life span before burning out completely.

Interplanetary debris

Countless smaller objects, ranging in size from dust grains to substantial boulders, also fill the space between the planets. Much of this material is blasted off asteroids when they collide with each other or is left behind in the tails of comets. When a chunk of this debris runs into Earth's atmosphere, the result is a shooting star or meteor—a bright trail of light given off as atmospheric friction heats the particle until it glows, then burns away to nothing. If the object is large enough, it may reach Earth's surface as a meteorite. In extreme cases, it may even form an impact crater.

There are several different types of meteorites. Some are metallic and obviously originated from the cores of larger protoplanets. Other meteorites have apparently not changed since they originally stuck together in the solar nebula, and a few can be linked to other worlds—such as the Moon and Mars. Meteorites provide a unique opportunity for astronomers to study the composition of the early solar system and to learn more about the conditions that gave birth to our own planet.

GLOSSARY

accrete: to collect additional material (often in a disk), such as when a star pulls in gas and dust from space or another object.

acid rain: rain, snow, fog, or mist that has absorbed chemicals from the atmosphere and falls with a slightly acidic pH.

astronomy: the scientific study of the universe, including the planets, moons, stars, and beyond.

atmosphere: an envelope of gases surrounding a planet or other celestial body.

atmospheric refraction: the bending of light rays as they pass through Earth's atmosphere; often causes astronomical objects to appear higher or larger.

centennial: a one-hundredth anniversary.

infrared: invisible form of radiation given off by high temperature objects; also called heat radiation.

meteorite: an object that enters the Earth's atmosphere from space and passes through it to strike the ground.

molten: melted; liquefied by heat.

nebula: a cloud of gas or dust in space that forms between the stars or surrounds a star.

protoplanet: a whirling mass of gas within a gigantic cloud of gas and dust that rotates around a sun and eventually becomes a planet.

solar: of or relating to the sun.

solar system: a set of celestial objects, including a star, its planets and moons, and all other bodies that are held in place by that star's gravity as they orbit around it.

spectrum: an ordered arrangement that can be broken down into its many components.

subduction: the sliding of one tectonic plate under another; caused by density differences and the internal pressures of a planet.

synchronous: taking place, existing, or arising at exactly the same time.

tectonics: the geological forces that shape a planet's crust and cause folds and faults.

terrestrial: belonging to the group of planets that are like Earth in density and composition. Venus, Mars, and Mercury are terrestrial planets.

ultraviolet: invisible electromagnetic radiation with wavelengths shorter than visible light but longer than X-rays.

FURTHER INFORMATION

BOOKS

Angelo, Joseph A. *Encyclopedia of Space Exploration*. Facts on File Science Library (2000).

Graun, Ken. *Our Earth and the Solar System*. Ken Press (2000).

Evert, Laura. *Planets, Moons, and Stars*. Northwood Press (2003).

Mars. DK Children (2004).

Ride, Sally. *Exploring Our Solar System*. Crown Books (2003).

Saturn. DK Children (2004).

Sparrow, Giles (Ed.). *The Solar System: Exploring the Planets and Their Moons, from Mercury to Pluto and Beyond*. Thunder Bay Press (2006).

Sparrow, Giles, Exploring the Solar System series, Heinemann, 2001

Stott, Carole. *Stars and Planets*. Kingfisher (2005).

WEB SITES

www.nasa.gov
Check out NASA's latest missions and activites.

www.space.com
Visit the best Web site for daily space news.

http://space.jpl.nasa.gov
Choose your view of the solar system from any angle or time.

www.nineplanets.org
Take a multimedia tour of the solar system.

http://solarsystem.nasa.gov/kids/
Surf NASA's solar system exploration pages.

Publisher's note to educators and parents: Our editors have carefully reviewed these Web sites to ensure that they are suitable for children. Many Web sites change frequently, however, and we cannot guarantee that a site's future contents will continue to meet our high standards of quality and educational value. Be advised that children should be closely supervised whenever they access the Internet.

INDEX

accretion 10
Adams, John Couch 37
aphelion 8
Arecibo 10–11
Ariel 36
asteroids 5, 10, 39, 40–41

basalt rocks 26
Brahe, Tycho 9

calendars 14
Callisto 32
Caloris Basin 23
carbon dioxide 28
Cassini Division 33, 34
Cassini Probe 35
celestial police 40–41
Ceres 40, 41
chaotic terrain 23
Charon 38, 40
Christy, James 40
Clementine 18
comets 10, 39, 43–45
Copernicus, Nicolaus 9
craters 18

Dione 33

Earth 12–16
    atmosphere 10, 13
    core 26
    gravity 21
    orbit 8
    water cycle 13, 45
eclipses 15–16
Einstein, Albert 14
electromagnetic spectrum (EM) 8,
    10–11
Enceladus 33
Encke 44
Europa 32

Galilei, Galileo 9, 18, 32
Galle, Johann 37
gamma rays 8, 10, 11
Ganymede 32
giant planets 9–10, 30–37
Giotto 44
Grand Canyon 28
Great Red Spot 32

Halley's Comet 44
Herschel, John 41
Herschel, William 5, 37
Hopkins Ultraviolet Telescope 11
Hubble Space Telescope (HST) 11, 41
hydrogen 31

Iapetus 33
ice dwarfs 39, 41
ice giants 35–37
inferior planets 6
interplanetary debris 45
Io 5, 32
IR (infrared) waves 8, 10

Juno 41
Jupiter 30–33
    comets 35
    Great Red Spot 32
    moons 5, 9, 32–33
    orbit 9

Kepler, Johannes 9
Kirkwood gaps 41
Kuiper Belt 6, 40, 41–42

late heavy bombardment 18
lunar months 15
Lunik 3 18

maria 18
Mariner 9 27–28
Mariner 10 22, 24
Mars 26–28
    atmosphere 28
    canals 29
    life 28–29
    moons 8–9
    orbits 8
    surfaces 22
    volcanoes 26
Mars Spirit Rover 22
Maxwell, James Clerk 33
Mercury 23–24
    core 26
    orbit 6, 23
meteorite ALH84001 28–29
meteorites 45
meteors 45
microwaves 8
Mimas 33
Miranda 36
Moon 14–21
    far side 19
    mapping 19
    orbit 14–15, 21
    origins 16
    phases 15
    size 8, 14
    surface 16–19
    tides 19–21

Near-Earth Asteroids 41
Neptune 35–37
    discovery 5, 37
    moons 9
    orbit 9
    rings 36

Oberon 36
Olympus Mons 26, 28
Oort Cloud 10, 11, 42, 43
orbits 6–9
outer planets 9–10, 30–37

Pallas 40–41
perihelion 8
Phoebe 33
Pioneer Venus 25
planets, definitions 5–6

Pluto 39–41
    discovery 5–6
    orbit 6, 9, 39
protoplanets 10, 11

radar waves 8
radiation 8
radio telescopes 10–11
radio waves 8
relativity 14
Rhea 33
rings 9, 33, 34–35, 36

Saturn 33–35
    moons 9, 33–34
    orbit 9
    rings 9, 33, 34
Schiaparelli, Giovanni 29
seasons 14
Sedna 42
shooting stars 45
shepherd moons 33
solar nebulae 10–11
solar systems 7, 10–11
Special Theory of Relativity 14
speed of light 8, 14
Spitzer Space Telescope 11
Sputnik 11
subduction 27
Sun 10–11

tectonic plates 14, 26–27
telescopes 10–11, 41
terrestrial planets compared 26–27
Tethys 33
Tharsis Bulge 26, 27
tides 15, 19–21
Titan 9, 33–35
Titania 36
Titius-Bode Law 40–41
Tombaugh, Clyde 39
Triton 36–37
Trojans 41

Umbriel 36
Uranus 35–37
    discovery 5
    moons 9, 36
    orbit 9, 35
    rings 36
UV (ultraviolet) waves 8, 10, 11

Valles Marineris 27–28
Venus 24–26
    cores 26
    orbits 6, 25
    tectonic plates 26
Vesta 41
volcanoes 14, 25–27
Voyager 1 12
Voyager 2 32, 35

water cycle 13, 45
white spots 33

X-rays 8, 10, 11

DEMCO